Setting Up A Making Food Catering Business

Your Guidebook To Food Preparation, Food Delivery And Affordable Party Planning So You Can Serve Up Great Food and Offer Great Service For Weddings, Birthdays, Christmas Or Any Event For A Real Party Treat!

Katrina P. Votswana
Copyright 2010

The major elements of any catering business are the food and service. After all, any event, whether for business or social function, requires a selection of food and drinks and some amount of service to do the job of organizing the food and drinks for the event or meeting.

However, the business of food catering is more than just cooking and food and drinks selection. It also calls for the very basic administrative tasks, financial planning, marketing and sales, as well as public relations activities.

Word of mouth marketing is still the most powerful form of advertising, so you would definitely want to set up your start-up business with the right fundamentals so you're all ready for progress. You may want to take into account some of these important business strategies when setting up your food catering business:

1. Study your target market, which are your potential customers and potential competitors
2. Write down your business plan covering all possible challenges to success
3. Securing your finances
4. Taking care of business registration and documentation
5. Personnel, inventory and daily management

A food catering business can be a very lucrative business idea nowadays. If managed well, a small start-up home-based business can easily turn into a big-time, top-choice pick of any business or social activity.

Table of Contents

Introduction

Anyone can easily get lost in the world of cooking is it for large families, small twosomes or even cooking for profit. Sometimes, one can get so engrossed in cooking that it may become hard to adapt to cooking small portions as when cooking a romantic meal for two. It need not mean cutting down on the looks of the meal; just knowing what is essential to cooking a good meal should suffice. You will certainly need to find the best available recipes and then are inspired into making sumptuous meals.

Every Cook Has To Start Somewhere

Cooking tips are what can help you out in different situations as even the best chefs will tell you, every cook has to start somewhere. So, you can begin by selecting a recipe that is not too complicated, especially when you are a beginning cook. Having selected the recipe, make sure you read it from start to finish and have on hand the right ingredients, utensils as well as appliances and also understand the directions.

Having obtained and read your recipe, you will now need some more cooking tips to master the meals that you are going to cook, which means letting your creative juices flow freely. It may mean experimenting with all kinds of ingredients and also using herbs as well as spices as also being artistic, and trying out different colors and textures.

Some more cooking tips that will help include preparing what is necessary prior to starting your cooking endeavor, and also using a broiler to cook your steaks as well as pre-heating the oven till it gets nice and hot which will help in searing the meat from outside as well as hold the juices within.

Another useful cooking tip is to get a potato ricer to use for mashed potatoes, and this wonderful gadget that appears just like a giant garlic press and which you can buy for just six dollars will make for some very smooth and airy mashed potatoes. Besides, when grilling your food, you will also be able to learn of some important cooking tips such as making sure that you grill meat as well as your vegetables by placing them four inches from the heat source, and keeping chicken six to eight inches away. If you want more flavors, then add pre-soaked chunks of hickory and other natural hardwoods.

And, if you are baking potatoes, you will find many cooking tips such as using potato with high starch so that you get puffed up baked potatoes. Also, search out and find potatoes that are smooth as well as are devoid of sprouts and avoid potatoes with wrinkled skins or soft spots. And, come Thanksgiving and you will need some cooking tips on cooking your Turkey. Thankfully, there are many cooking tips that you can use such as deciding what kind of turkey to cook is it fresh, frozen, natural etc. and then knowing the best method of cooking such as roasting, grilling, barbequing as well as more.

The world of cooking is quite exhaustive and were it not for cooking tips, one would be hard pressed into getting the most out of the experience.

The Business Of Food

One of the greatest types of business to start up by anyone is the catering business since it is considered as one of the most profitable while also having a high potential for expansion and growth. It is extremely rewarding for the person starting up, and can also be considered as to being a lot of fun. There are many different events that take place in your current neighborhood which you may not know yourself; all of these events contain the opportunity for you to provide your catering services to them. These events, which you should already start focusing on, can be considered birthday parties for adults or even birthday parties for children. Catering services have expended in many different ways and it remains a very profitable type of business for everyone.

Starting a catering business, or rather any other type of business involves a lot of risk. Not only will you have to get ready to devote most or all of your time into the business in the beginning in order to be successful and achieve the goals you have set for yourself, but you will also be risking the investment money which you will be spending throughout the life of the business. These risks and thoughts go through every business minded person before they decide to put their thoughts into action. This e-book will be covering almost every aspect in order for you to feel reassured that you will and you can establish a successful catering business. This e-book is not only written to motivate you and give you some reassurance, but rather it is to benefit you throughout the life of your catering business.

Setting Up The Business Plan

The first thing which you should keep in mind is what you actually want to accomplish with your catering business. The procedure of starting your own catering business is not so difficult; you must first however come up with a plan. The idea of developing a business from scratch is to first develop a sense of what you wish to do.

One of the first thing which you must recognize is the fact whether you would like to work full-time or rather on a part-time basis. Every other person has different responsibilities and requirements that must be met before hand. That is the first thing which you should consider, since working full time will have more a demand on yourself.

It is important to not think of the catering business as too easy, which many people originally do. If it was easy, everyone would be doing it. If you believe you have the required stamina to meet the demanding work as well as the ability to work well and effectively under stress and pressure while maintain a great or excellent sense of talking with your customers and their guests, then perhaps it is something which you may be capable of accomplishing.

Another great idea which you may want to keep under consideration is the fact that you will need to create a great reputation for yourself in this line or work, while also being able to maintain that reputation by fulfilling all of your customers' needs. This means that you must be extremely hard working in order to maintain that reputation, and you must be ready to be willing to work under the stress. We will be talking about how you can manage the stress from work later on.

Many people first start off with starting a catering business from their home. In this way, they will be the head chef and responsible for all actions while also having a larger responsibility on your own part to meet the customers' demands. This is a very interesting and great idea to start off with since you will not have any overhead expense, and you will be getting paid for your own labor and work.

Work At Home Catering Business

This type of business is becoming very rapid in its growth and is becoming more and more popular with many people and all different types of regions as well as people with different income levels. The reason is due to the increased demand in this type of business over the recent few years. If you were to do the research yourself, you would easily see that the figures speak for themselves. The actual boom of this market started in the 1999 to 2000 when it increased by nearly a 5.7% in sales reaching nearly $3.6 billion in just the United States. This impressive figure was taken through the National Restaurant Association's 2000 Restaurant Industry Forecast. This figure also provides the fact which proves the great underestimated demand of this marketplace.

Starting this type of business from your home is not as difficult as many people have assumed it to be; it requires a few things and needs a few certain characteristics. These characteristics are mainly the way you manage yourself in order to run this business, since you will be required to spend your own time and money into it. Most of all, you will be required to adjust your work schedule with your home schedule while staying under the same roof, which is sometimes considered to be a hard thing to accomplish by some people.

Starting up from your own house will have very little start up costs for you to endure. Catering from your house compared to establishing a traditional restaurant and catering will require a lot less initial investment or capital. Depending on how much potential investment or capital you have, you can plan to start off according to that size. If the kitchen you are already working in has all the required essentials, then your start up costs will be a lot less. However, if you wish to get more you can go into the wide ranging category of spending nearly $1,000 on just the essentials that you require, as well as going up to $80,000 for a complete professional touched kitchen.

Even by working from home, you first have to figure out if you want to maintain an office from home while cooking from home or you could just maintain an office from home while having some type of mobile kitchen for you to be able to cook at the locations of your customer right at the spot. Sometimes, in the beginning, most caterers provide low prices in order to use the facilities or kitchen of the client or at the place that the event is taking place. The final touches can be prepared at these places, but the initial starting prep work for these dishes must be taken into consideration and be completed prior to going to the customer's house or the place where the event is being held. These prep works can be something minor, such as cutting up vegetables and placing them in zip lock bags in order to use your time more efficiently, to readying an entire dish which is ready for baking.

By being able to be flexible in this manner, by being ready to cook away from your home, you will be cutting down your initial costs extremely. The reason that you want to cut down on any start up costs or any overhead is that it benefits your clients when you are charging them for your services. If you have a large overhead, which you need to keep in consideration, you will have to carry that expense over in order to make sure that you are eventually breaking even if not making profit. You must remember to keep in consideration the value of your own time and labor which you have spent when charging your customers.

Major Considerations

In order to maintain and run a small catering business from your own home, you will need a lot more than just the passion for being able to cook great tasting dishes. You will need to start managing your own time and plan your events carefully. There will be a large need of organization skills while staying flexible to any last minute changes that may occur, since they occur in a very frequent amount in this type of business. Along with that, your personal needs will require for you to be able to have a type of intuition in order to manage and see what it is that people are enjoying since there are so many different cultural and environmental standards.

Not only will you be required to provide your customer and their guests with a satisfying taste in all of your dishes, but also the way you prepare, show, and serve your food is extremely important. It must be presented in a manner where it leaves your clients and their guests in a pleasant state of mind even after they have experienced your food. This means that you must also focus on the different plate styles and culinary essentials while presenting them, as well as the selection of venue which you have to offer, along with the table decors that are readily available by you. Anything which you can do to remain and maintain a unique catering business will end up being more of a benefit to you compared to the rest of the similar competition out there. Overall, you must be prepared to be able to provide a service which keeps your customer's happy as well as always coming back to you for more of your services.

There is no special type of education or training which you will be required to go through in order to remain a successful person in the catering business. However, there are many courses that are available in different institutes and schools which can increase and help you to achieve your desired results, while also giving you what you may need. Often times, by working at another catering business, you may be able to easily see and get an inside look as to how to manage and make the business prosper over the lifetime of the business.

This type of business, the catering service, requires you to be extremely well planned and to be able to work according to that plan while also being flexible enough to adjust your plan for any obstacles or problems that may arise. The success of this business is directly related to the amount of effort you are willing to put in order to maintain those few ideas. You must be easily able to understand exactly what the customers are wanting while they are trying to describe to you what it is; you must provide your customers with a sense of knowledge which others may lack. This is what makes you different and better from the competition out there.

Besides the fact that these benefits are extremely logical and can be taken advantage of, you can easily start planning and seeing how this new business of yours is affecting your own personal life at home with your family. This is a great thing to keep in mind when deciding on whether you should continue or you should stop. If you see that there are no problems arising within your own family life that you cannot overcome, perhaps you may want to reconsider or readjust your schedule to make it more convenient for everyone in the household.

Income Potential

The amount of income that one can make in this line of business is entirely up to the person in charge of running this business. With the amount of effort and free time that you have available, you may be able to start catering depending on the size of the actual event, the amount of people that are come, as well as the type of event it may be. These factors put together, along with the proper advertising, can determine a successful catering business from an unsuccessful one.

Just like many other businesses out there in the today's world, catering requires several people to be on their upmost performance when it comes to management and organizational skills. These skills come in handy when you are ready to offer others an extremely high quality service with the proper and fair price compared to the rest of t he competition. Along with that, proper management and organizational skills can lead you to keep your operating costs at a minimum while also causing the least bit of stress for yourself.

Depending on how fast you want to see the return of your investment, you can easily get an estimate time period by figuring out the initial investment. Obviously, the larger the investment in the initial starting stages, the better off your business will strive in less amount of time. If you choose to start this business from almost no type of investment, you will be seeing some type of return and savings but obviously much later on as you would. This is entirely up to you to decide how much you actually want to spend into this business.

Remember that any business is like you planting a tree. First thing you need to do in order to plant a tree is to actually find a spot. Once you've found that spot, you have to decide what type of tree you want to grow and also calculate if the location of the tree will change the settings in your yard in a positive or a negative manner. Once you have decided the type of tree you want, you have to go out and actually get either some seeds or maybe even a smaller tree and then plant it in and keep nurturing it until its roots start developing into the ground.

The amount of time and effort you put into your business, especially your catering business, is in a direct correlation with the amount of money you make. The amount of investment you choose to go through with, is also in direct correlation with the amount of time it will take for you to see that profit and income arising. If you feel more secure starting off your business with a small capital, perhaps you should do that if you are comfortable with the fact that the time of return will be much slower. If you wish to see the revenue arriving at a much faster and sooner time, then perhaps you may want to arrange for some investment money in order to start up. Again, like many other things in this business, it is entirely up to you to decide as to how you want to proceed with your business.

As for a rough idea to see how much money is actually available in the catering business, a rough idea of an average caterer in a city, or any large metropolitan area, can easily have sales which reach up towards $200,000 in just a year. While someone doing the exact same business from their home, on a part time basis or during just seasons, then they could expect to make nearly $50,000 in a year. Even then, it is a great amount to expect if it is managed and organized well and if you plan on doing this just part time.

Where To Costs-Cut

There are many different ways to start cutting down your costs initially. By being able to cut down these costs, you will eventually be able to provide a service to your clients at a much more reasonable rate compared to the competition out there. In order to first

You can even cut down your costs by renting certain items which you require instead of purchasing them in a large sum. Certain things which you may be able to rent from a local store might be the use of kitchen facilities to the utensils that are used, as well as tables and the tablecloths that can be used at these events. There is a large benefit behind being able to rent these items in the beginning compared to actually owning them.

The reason that one should consider renting them in the beginning is that logically, you will be saving a lot of money. Until you start seeing a steady amount of revenue coming into your hands, you should not consider expanding. Slowly and slowly, as you are gathering your revenue, you can start expanding by purchasing some materials and equipment. We will be covering as to how you can expand further easily while maintain a steady amount of profit. In order to maintain a steady amount of profit, you must be able to keep the reputation which you have built for yourself as a caterer, while building that reputation you can easily start to do so by developing and saving some money in order to use it for an investment later on.

Another benefit of renting equipment is the fact that you can easily view and see what it is that you will require as an essential tool for your business and what it is that you can do without immediately. You can create a list of the items which may make catering more efficient for you. This is a great way to experiment and see what is working for you as well as what isn't working for you.

Besides being able to rent equipment, you will be saving a lot of money by using your own house as your own personal office. Instead of having to cover the expenses of rent or any additional necessity bills, you can easily decide to and work from your home in a rewarding manner.

Along with the ideas mentioned above, another great idea for you to try to do is to hire employees on a basis of when you will need them according to the catering events and pay them according to the events that they participate in. Obviously if you will be doing this part time, then you would have to explain the situation and timing to them as well as a very quick and short summary of what they are expected to accomplish when it comes to work. By being able to hire these employees on the dates of when you need their help on the days of these events, you will be able to find a lot of help who would be willing to help. The best types of employees to have, for these weekend night events, are college students as well as any other type of student.

The idea of renting a kitchen elsewhere, or using your clients' kitchen would save a lot of money. You could prepare your food at home and have it so that it would be ready to cook in any kitchen and be served right away.

Depending on the nature of your style of the catering business, you can easily go on and off per seasons. You can decide to serve only at weddings and start your catering business for three or four months during the season which you think is best for weddings. In that scenario, you would not need to hire a large number of employees that you must keep and pay all year around.

The main thing to keep in mind is the effect it will place on your service and reputation that you provide to your clients and their guests. The service you provide for your clients must not be risked nor should it be played around with, it should be maintained at its peak performance throughout the course of interaction with your clients.

Licensing

Another thing to be aware of is that some countries as well as some states require for there to be a catering business license that must be somehow managed and received by you. Even then, sometimes these caterers have a way of providing and serving alcohol and some events, even then you would require a license in most of the states within the United States.

The license is not hard to receive and only takes a little bit of time or dedication on your own part, the only reason it is there is to make sure that not every person is able to enter this market and exploit it. You must make sure with your local city government what your catering business requires. These license numbers, where enforced, are to be displayed on your own business cards as well as on any type of advertising you have in order to stay within the boundaries of the law.

Promoting And Advertising

There are many different ways for you to start advertising your catering business right away. The best method, and the most efficient method, is the approach of actually talking to people face to face and explaining to them your services and why your services are going to be better than the rest of the competition out there. This way, any time they plan on setting an event and wonder how much food or how much they will need to spend for that event, they will instantly think about you and contact you in order for you to quote them a price. After you have quoted them a price, and proven your reputation and service to them, anytime their friends have any events that they are starting to schedule, they would recommend you. The best way to get recommendations from these customers is to actually ask for it. A simple request for making some referrals to their friends and family is a great way to start.

The next major thing which you have to accomplish is to be able to provide a type of business card with your business name, your business license, and a contact number. These business cards can be printed yourself as well as printed professionally. The latest trend of getting these business card printed online and shipped is the cheapest and most efficient method. All you would have to do is design the card yourself or use an available template that is readily available on a website.

Besides the idea of business cards, you would have to somehow get your message through to your customers. You could start that off by easily starting a website. A website with your rates and contact information as well as some details as to what makes you different from to other catering businesses is an essential tool in today's market.

Now, this is extremely important to keep in mind, if you plan on starting this business from home and only doing this part time then perhaps some of these ideas will not be suitable for you. These are just some general ideas which you may have or may not have considered yourself.

Along with a professional website and a business card, you can easily hand out a type of brochure or pamphlet that you can hand to people while explaining them to you in a very quick and short summary of what it is that you have to offer them. This way you will be contacting people face to face, while keeping advertising expenses down to a bare minimum. This is a great tool to use when you are trying to grow your business in your own local neighborhood. Going from door to door to your neighbors and handing them brochures along with your business cards is extremely profitable in the long run. The benefit is simple, all it requires is the cost of printing and your own labor that you may either hire or that you may do yourself. This way you will create a short rapport with people that they will be able to remember when they are deciding on who they should hire for their catering needs.

Essentially, depending on how much you want to invest and what results your desire to witness, you can easily pick any method that you believe most useful and start getting your message out. The first type of people you would like to contact are ones which in your own neighborhood or previous contacts that you may have made, this includes all and any type of relative.

Computing Prices For Catering Packages

The price charged for the catering service is very important. Many people don't purchase the catering service because it will cost them money. But, if someone wants to have a good event with good quality food, they should get the service of hiring a caterer and it is entirely up to you as to how you convince and present them with that information.

Pricing your customers is not as difficult as it seems. There are some important things which you need to calculate in order to price efficiently, they are mainly four important things. The price for materials, which includes the cost of foods as well as beverages that will be used is the first one. The price of the overhead costs that you must be ready to pay, this includes vehicle expense, rental expense, as well as the essential parts of maintaining and running a proper thriving business. The next thing which you should calculate is the cost of labor. The labor that you need and have hired for the event is extremely important. Lastly, you charge whatever profit you think is reasonable and acceptable. This is the part which you must remain to be flexible when you are dealing with your customer. You can always lower the profit in order to close a deal and make a sale so that you can get the work. Even if you have to make a little bit less than what you had expected, at least you will be able to use that time and use it to your advantage by being able to advertise to the client's guests.

In order to be successful in this business, you must be able to negotiate well and learn how to negotiate well. The key to this business is to please and meet your customer's satisfaction as long as they are reasonable.

Business Management Skills

Now that we've covered what you must expect and what you might need and want to do in order to start up this type of business, you can easily start trying to find the right help.

The right help is not just hiring the right people, but it has to do with how much preparing and what type of skills you want to tune or learn.

Most of all the right help is pretty much how you take care of yourself. How you manage your own time, how you hire the right staff, as well as how you manage stress. Understanding the causes of stress can make someone aware as to how important it is to actually take stress and use it in an efficient manner.

This chapter talks about the different things which you can easily do in order to make sure that you remain efficient in order to maximize your profit while also increasing the rate of customer satisfaction.

Culinary Expertise

Culinary classes are held at certain schools where they try to teach the education and the art, as well as the science, behind food preparation. There are certain types of classes and requires a certain amount of determination in order to continue with these classes.

The real question that some people ask is if these classes do help. The answer is simple; it may depend on the type of person.

If you are starting this career and you have managed to see a type of profit and want to learn fresh ideas as to how to present and make your own food as well as to manage it in a manner where it is more efficient, then perhaps it may be suitable for you. These classes not only teach you how to cook, but how to present a service to your clients in a way where you satisfy the needs of your clients.

Some of these classes are often associated and linked with public restaurants and thus allow for students to gain a little bit of experience since you can easily work in a professional field in the related environment. This can be a great way to learn the various roles that need to be performed in order to remain efficient and thus allow you to modify these roles according to your own standards.

Overall, these culinary classes may only be helpful to some people whereas to some people it may just be a sense of some general knowledge. If you have the option and can afford to take these classes, then perhaps you should consider doing so in order to learn something new about the market which you will be directly involved in.

Tips On Cooking Classes

There are many places offering cooking classes, though before choosing one particular one it would make good sense to choose the one that benefits you most. With a wide variety of cooking classes to choose from it may not always be that simple to find the best suited one though you can follow a few guidelines and tips in selecting the one that rises above the rest.

Size Of Class

To begin with, it is important to look at the size of the class and opt for cooking classes that have not many students in the class and about ten to twelve students would be ideal for your class. Too many students would lead to difficulties in hearing and seeing what is going on, while too few would mean less camaraderie with the other students.

You should also take the trouble of finding out whether the menu that different cooking classes provide is interesting to you as well as appeals to your senses. Also, you will be looking for clear as well as concise instructions that will help you finish up with a clear understanding of all that it takes to cook well, and which will thus enable you to replicate the lessons while cooking at home.

You will also want a copy of the recipes being taught and opt for those cooking classes that allow you to take home a copy of the recipes. Otherwise, you will be left with nothing but your memory to rely on, which means that you could forget important steps of your recipe and thus fail to get the full benefit from your learning experience.

The ideal cooking class should also be one that has a proper room setup in which every student has a clear view of what is going on, as rooms with traditional setups may cause a student to miss out on what is being taught. It would be better to have a room in a half circle with seating around the instructor that will keep each student at an equal distance from the teacher, and thus promote better learning.

Another important aspect to enrolling in a good cooking class is that there should be enough food offered in the class so that every student gets a chance to sample the menu. It would also be worthwhile trying out a cooking class that allows its students to prepare meals in the class since they will get the advantage of having the instructor help out on many matters relating to preparing good food.

Finally, and certainly not the least, is the importance of getting quality instruction in your cooking classes. A good instructor should be able to provide clear as well as concise as well as knowledgeable instructions, and the instructor must be able to answer all questions in an adequate manner and be a good communicator as well. You don't want to attend cooking classes in which the instructor uses terminology which you do not understand.

Time Management Skills

When you own a small business, such as a catering service, there are a lot of activities that need to be taken care of in a very short amount of time. The most difficult part for the caterer is staying focused and going in one direction. When there is a huge amount of work to be done, the pressure can scatter your focus and leave us mentally and physically drained. When the day ends, you actually wonder if you have achieved your goals for that day.

When you feel like you're headed in this direction you should stop right there and take a very deep breath. Remember that this business is to help you provide a service, not to make you a helpless wreck. If you started a catering business, that means that you chose to do what you love which is to be in control of things. To keep everything under control you must keep your cool and stay focused on the tasks at hand. The only way to keep your cool and stay focus is to stay on task and keeping yourself busy. This is how you will manage your time efficiently and effectively.

We all have the same amount of time each and every day. There is only 24 hours and no matter how hard you try the clocks will tick the same way no matter where you live. Time management techniques help us get the most out of every second. Becoming a master of this art will turn anyone into an efficient, productive, and inspirational person. There are many ways to lighten your workload. This will help you get more time out of the day.

Now for a catering business, the first step you should take is to go over your daily planner. See if it too large or to hectic. Look for the primary and crucial activities and make it your goal to accomplish all of them. Makes sure these are goals that need to be met. Now, what is let can probably wait if there is time or try to fit them in tomorrow. Now, when you have set aside your primary goals from the ones that can wait, you should list them in order from most important to the least important. As your day progresses, check your list and see that all your appointments, meetings, arrangements, and orders are being met. This will help your catering business beat all the competitors and you will stay focused and motivated. When you now that you are achieving your goals you will stay motivated and complete all the tasks efficiently and on time. If some other tasks pop up and need to be taken care of, you can just mix them in with your current schedule and/or put them aside for a time when you might be available.

Many business owners combine their business and personal activities and plan them all in one planner/list. However, experts recommend that there should be separate lists, one for business and one for personal activities. Try your best to avoid mixing your personal agenda during work hours, especially if you own a catering business.

Last minute changes can put a lot of pressure on caterers. If you are dealing with a client that has a big party or wedding where there is a possibility where the clientele might order more food or invite more people. This can put you in a huge pickle. So to avoid this before hand, you need to make sure that your clients are completely sure about what they want. If you're clients are unsure and indecisive, trying to help them with their plans with this in mind would be wasting time. So your first step would be to help make sure that the clients make up their mind and decide how they want their arrangements for their party.

If you think there are some customers that are wasting your time or if they are having trouble making up their minds, you can have someone else deal with them in the mean time. This is where hired help comes in handy. If you feel that your business is expanding then you are going to need a deeper staff. However, you should only hire more help only if you can really afford to do so. This will relieve you of some of your duties and lighten the load of work.

These are some ways to help you manage your time. This will expand your business and it will make you a much better and efficient person.

Efficiency

Stress is a symptom which can be caused by many different things and situations going around in your life, it can be due to family problems and even the problems faced at work. Many people, at their workplace feel a great amount of stress when a large amount of demands are put on them, and when their work is piled up to a great extent that a person feels stressed out. Another way people take on stress is when they plan on opening or starting their own business or company

Stress is very bad and very unhealthy as it can cause many problems later on including the damaging of arteries and it may cause high blood pressure. Stress also might put a person under a great risk of heart problem and may lead to depression and anxiety.

In our daily working life stress is a normal thing and it mostly depends on the way the person experiencing the stress handles it and interprets it. When one is under stress they reduce the performance as we use this mental effort in handling them, and stress therefore causes a lot of unhappiness in one's life and makes their life unbalanced in many ways.

When faced with such a great amount of stress many people try to break through this by drinking or smoking, and immediately get relief from stress. But this method of controlling stress is very bad and dangerous. When going through stress man y people stop eating and sleeping properly, they get so carried away in their work that they forget their daily needs and wants, and harm their health badly. They also do not get the required amount of sleep which a person should have to remain healthy, and so carry more stress on themselves.

One of the many jobs that cause a great amount of stress includes the great catering businesses. In the catering business the most important thing is to make sure the customers satisfaction is there. This is a stress causing moment when the clients order or wants are being done, or when the client is not happy with the outcome of the event organization. Due to this, stress will take over and no job will be done correctly or efficiently. To overcome this stress you have to be calm at all times and do not panic over the slightest mistake that is being made. One should learn to use this negative stress and convert it into positive stress and at the same time be able to work well under stress. This can be done by not getting under the pressure so much and to go with the flow.

You should be able to tell your clients that their catering needs are going to be taken care of and that they do not have to worry. To manage this stress and work great with it you should be able to use this stress along with the deadline and the perfection needed by putting the pressure of the deadline in your mind. By doing this you now know that you have a given amount of time to finish a particular job and that it needs to be done. So for unmotivated workers this pressure technique works best. You can also start planning for each clients request ahead of time so that you are more organized and feel less stressed when the deadline approaches.

Another huge stress factor is that carried on from the amount of money needed to be able to start your catering business and to be able to make it grow. To overcome this stress the creator of this business should have enough money in advance to keep their business running smoothly for the first few months or even the first few years. To be able to control this stress one should take up activities that give you peace. For instance taking up exercising is a good way to handle the stress you are feeling.

One big issue comes from the chaotic attitude of catering and the hectic deadlines which have to be followed through to be able to call ones business successful and to fulfill the costumers' wants and needs. To deal with this stress one should try breathing exercises which help in the relaxation of the mind and body.

One of the many ways of releasing stress is by putting more fun and stress removing activities into your daily routine so you can counter-balance the amount of stress carried on, and replace some of it by healthy and active activities. While working a job in the catering business in which stressful and chaotic circumstances are taking place, one might work extra hours and cut down on vacations, and also on their sleep to be able to work around with more time, and this can be very bad for health.

You should learn how to put this negative stress and convert it into something more positive. It is a proven fact that if one is put under an amount of pressure or stress, the demands put on them with the catering tasks ,with deadlines which would help to motivate them to get the work done. They also may be able to interpret this stress from a negative view to a more positive view which would single handedly solve the problem of stress. When a very lazy or under motivated person is working, they will not do any work until the deadline approaches and the excessive amount of stress is put on them, and then the work is completed. So these are some of many ways how stress can be positive.

After entering the catering business and after facing the stress there are many ways to deal with the stress which includes by putting more fun and stress removing activities into your daily routine so you can counter-balance the amount of stress carried on, and replace some of it by healthy and active activities. One of the big things needed to lower stress is rest and relaxing, we need rest at the end of the day so that you become calmer and can cope with the stress led on by your newly developed catering business in a much better and healthier manner. When a person does more things that involve the family or friends they bring back a little bit of balance in their life especially if they experience stress more and if it has become a routine for them to go through these unpleasant levels of stress.

Another good way of releasing stress after staring your new catering business is by taking up enjoyable and non-rushing, peaceful sports or finding some kind of hobby which fits you correctly. After spending a long day at work one should be able to come home after that hectic day at work, trying to fulfill your clients' wants and should be able to relax a bit by doing slow physical activities such as walking, sailing or golf.

Another factor in the catering business that causes a great amount of stress is when a customer cancels their event and all the hard work put into that job is gone to waste and the money is taken back, the stress and pressure one feels is enormous and a great way of unwinding would be by watching television or reading a novel or socializing with people. It is also important to go on small vacations and be able to get away from the situation that you will go through once you go back to work and have to go through the same problem again.

Another important thing needed to be able to over cone stress would be by getting the appropriate time of sleep in one day. An average person gets about 8-11 hours of sleep a day, and if the amount of sleep is shortened then the concentration level declines and it is harder to concentrate on any work or task given. This will increase the stress and therefore one should get enough rest to keep them going normal throughout the day. If one skips a routine sleep they will make the bad situation even more difficult.

Stress is a very common thing, especially when you own a business and in this case a catering business which is very hectic and fast-paced; thus the stress should be dealt with in a proper manner. Stress is dealt with in different ways by usually exercising, yoga classes, breathing exercises, and just being able to let go of work for a while and enjoy with family and friends. This way you are able to understand why it is that you are running this business in the first place. Besides the fact of self satisfaction, you can understand that it is just a business and a means of making money, nothing more.

Providing a customer satisfaction should not come before your own health, ever. This is an extremely important fact which should be remembered by almost everyone in order to remain happy.

Hiring People

You can easily hire some help depending on how much help you may actually need. Depending on how you choose to go on with your catering business as well as how much you want to expand, you will be needing different roles and services in order to remain successful. This is also the best way to spread apart some of the stresses of this job and to actually be able to focus on what is more important. For instance, if you can afford to, perhaps you should hire a manager so that they can look after the staff while you are busy trying to gather new events and focus on expanding further. This way, you will not only be less stressed out on a daily basis, but you will also be able to focus your energy and time on how to get more work or something more helpful to working efficiently.

In order to be able to get the right staff, which is extremely important of running a proper business, you must be able to evaluate the interviewee within a matter of seconds on the first impression and see if that person can actually benefit your overall business instead of being a burden. Establishing a proper working staff is incredibly important in order to maintain a successful business. Especially in the beginning or while deciding to expand, since you will need to cut your expenses in order to maximize your profit, you are at a dilemma of choosing the proper staff.

How To Conduct The Interview

It's five minutes until three and you're getting ready to interview another kid that is probably shaking in his pants. You can imagine just what is going through his/her mind. Now you check the copy of the job description sitting on your desk. Make sure to write down all the questions you have to ask before going into the interview. Make sure you are prompt during the interview. When the candidate walks in, you start by introducing yourself. Now as you get past the introductions try to make the candidate feel comfortable by starting some small talk. Now if for any reason, you are unable to interview the candidate, be sure to inform them, even if you are going to take five extra minutes. If the candidates don't know why the interview is delayed then they stress out even more. It is very crucial that you communicate with the candidates if there is a delay. Don't let them think that they are not worth your time.

Now, as the interview is under way and a conversation has actually started, this when you start the actual interview. Have the candidate talk about his/her self. Try to relate to them if you can. While this is happening, you should be taking notes. This is a very common practice during interviews. Now, it is very crucial that you always maintain eye contact with the candidate. Make sure that there are no interruptions during your interview unless it is an emergency.

You can use the resume as an outline to help your evaluations during the interview. You can start with the candidates past and work up to the present or vice-versa.

When conducting an interview make sure that you touch on the qualities that meet the requirements of the job description. Ask some questions for example, have you ever used Microsoft word? Have you ever had to arrange a party or helped arrange a party?

Be careful when taking an interview. Do not overstep any legal boundaries when asking questions. You should make a list of legal ways of asking questions just in case. Take a look at the list once in a while and phrase your questions accordingly.

Be sure that you discuss the job requirements and qualifications with the candidate. Now this may seem silly but you have to ask them if they are interested in the position and why do they think they are qualified. Try to get them to expand themselves. If they aren't selling themselves at this point then they probably don't care about the job.

If there are other candidates waiting for their turn, then let the candidate that's being interviewed know about this. Give him or her certain amount of time and let them know that during this time frame you will be making your decision. If you have just recently started interviewing some possible candidates, it will be a little while be you make your final decision. Explain this to all the candidates so they don't get stressed out if you take a week or so.

Now, if you find the right candidate let them know how you feel and why you feel that way. Be sure to explain and other procedures that you need to complete during this time. This could be background checks, the references, drug tests, criminal record, etc. Give the candidate an estimated time frame. You have to be completely sure that this candidate really wants this job and will be happy doing it. Now if there is anything left to discuss like the salary, benefits, any other information, now would be the time to do so. Now if you both agree upon this, you have to go to the next step which would be to make sure that all the protocol and processes are taken care of such as the start date and time. It is a good idea to send the selected candidate an offer letter that points out every little detail that you have discussed. Include the job requirements, responsibilities, salary, start date, working hours, benefit packages, who to report to for any other conformation, etc. Once the letter has be signed by the candidate and delivered to you, you can welcome them and start the training.

Another great test which you can try to do in order to find the right help is to actually use a little tip which some great managers only know. When you are calling the interviewee back, you can easily state to them that perhaps they are not the right person for the job. If they agree or do not try to entertain the comment by defending themselves, then perhaps you are better off without that person on your team. A person who defends themselves and stands up and asks why not, as well as shows some persistence, is the right person that you want for the job.

Unique Catering Concepts

In order to remain a successful business, you must have something to offer which others aren't able to provide. The services you provide, as in the customer dealing and the customer satisfaction that you give, has to be extremely better so that they always remember the service that they received from you. This is a great way to separate yourself from your own competition. The few things which you have to ask yourself are what are missing from the competition and how can you make it better, as well as what do customers really want when they hire a caterer for their needs? These small little things added together make a large difference when it comes to customers remembering the people that they have done business with.

Another way you can be different is to actually focus on one event and just one event. In that manner, you will exactly be able to specify and understand the customers' needs as well as what is expected of you and what you should prepare for the event.

Many caterers have taken the option of becoming too involved with too much, perhaps that is a good thing when you have a large staff as well as a means of being efficient while providing a great service.

In the beginning however, you may think of focusing on just one type of event in order to be remembered by the clients as well as to for your services to be used or referred by their friends and family members.

Overall Goal

The overall goal that you want to try and achieve in this stage, of being different, is to basically leave the clients off in a stunned emotion where they were not expecting what you provided them. Of course this has to be in a good and positive manner otherwise it does not really provide you any future work from that specific client. The clients must be impressed by the minor things that you can provide them. These things can consist of just the basic essentials.

These small little things do really add up and make a large difference when it comes to catering since there is a very large and intense competition out there. Making and keeping the customers happy, you will not only be securing the return of the customers but also inviting their guests to use your services for any event that they might have.

Table Setting

For instance, depending on the type of presentation you choose to lay out for the plates according to the tables, as well as the way you lay out the utensils that are needed for the specific meal. You must remember not to place a steak knife when there is no steak on the venue. These minor things add up and end up leaving a positive impression on your clients.

Venue Recommendations

Another type of positive impression that you can leave is the vast venue selection that you may have to offer for your clients. If you are focusing on any one specific type of event, then this is a great opportunity for you to be able to explore and be able to provide the vast meals that are usually expected at these events.

The menu that you may provide to your customers should have a variety of foods that are acceptable to every type of customer. You must be able to offer your own opinion in a friendly manner since the customer will most likely be looking up to an expert for some advice as to how to deal with this. You must advice the client to be able to choose properly by explaining in detail the different texture, shape, sizes, cooking methods, colors, and flavor. The other main thing which you must be able to explain to them is the actual price of the item and why it is different from other food items on your menu.

There are certain things which you should focus on, and you can easily recommend the client to choose an eye appealing meal that has at least a few colorful foods to choose from, as well as ranging from different flavors.

Another little tip which you could follow is to provide our clients with a little sample prior to the event for them to make a decision on what type of food they actually want to serve at the wedding. This is a great way to take that extra little step in satisfying the customers' expectations and going beyond.

Decoration Ideas

In order to provide a great table decoration, which is part of the placement of utensils and plates, you must also provide the best color style according to their themes. Remember, caterers are not just bound to the food, but as well as the tables, chairs, as well as the coverings.

Some caterers have even gone to the extent of hiring professional artists to not only decorate in a professional manner, but also to use some additional equipment to leave the clients and their guests wowing. For example, some use professional pyrotechnics in order to provide a sense of uniqueness, as well as laser light shows while dinner is being served in order to give the clients and their guests an event which they have not witnessed before and one which they will not forget.

Specializing In Weddings Receptions

If you choose to focus on just weddings, then understanding what is the caterer's job at a wedding is extremely important as well as what type of foods, services, and environment must be set up in order to satisfy the customers' needs.

Most caterers have found that during a semiformal wedding, the best type of food which most guests appear to like is usually different types of sandwiches, cold cuts, cocktails foods, buffet style dishes, and a wedding cake, as well as some minor snacks to munch on during the wedding. Caterers try to make their customers and their guests happy by serving all types of different foods which are available and usually have become common at other weddings. People think that the buffet style meals are not as expensive and are cheaper compared to other types of food, they are incorrect. The cost is about the same or many times more expensive. Many caterers have to overestimate the food that will be eaten at the wedding. Due of this reason, the couple that has full control of the wedding end up being charged more than they actually would for a sit down meal. The caterer sends a bill according to how many people will be there. This means that the customer is then charged on a basis of each person that is attending the wedding.

The wedding reception is an important function, therefore the food is considered a major part of the wedding and all good weddings must have good caterers providing the best service possible.

At a semiformal American wedding, the beverages that are usually served are mainly alcoholic beverages. These beverages consist of champagne or a type of fruit punch for a toast, but mostly champagne is the most commonly used at these weddings overall. Most weddings have an open bar throughout the wedding. Soft drinks, juices, and different types of alcoholic beverages are served. Sometimes, at some weddings, a variety of wines are served by waiters to people that are attending the wedding and are further served at the guests' tables. This is done throughout the wedding by hired staff members.

Specializing In Business Lunches

Some caterers only provide lunches for businesses. In this sense you will be providing a quick and easy to eat lunch depending on the type of location you have. This is a great way to reach the target market in the executive area. Most of the people attending these business meetings are going to be expecting an extremely professional staff and tasty food.

Depending on the type of business meeting it is, either a room full of CEO's or stock holders, or just a large number of members of the sales team, as well as a promotion for the company towards the community, there are many different types of lunches and ideas which you can provide to them.

Overall, it has to be easy to eat, quick to eat, and something which they will always remember. Most caterers provide a type of a sandwich or a wrap which is easy to hand out and serve as well as easy to take care of while eating. Some caterers have gone to the extent of providing actual entrees where they provide chicken parmesan, lasagna, pot roast, baked ham. Again, it has to be something very simple to eat; otherwise there will be a major distraction and problem. There can also be some easy to eat sweets or desserts which can be brownies or cookies, something which doesn't require the usage of a lot of utensils in order to eat. You must remember to ask your client as to how many people are expected and what type of meeting this is in order to make sure you have the right type of food as well as the right staff.

Specializing In Birthday Events

Birthday parties for children are very common around the country and are usually a big hit for most caterers. Not all birthday parties require catering but if good food is wanted it is recommended that a birthday party does go through a caterer in order to be provided some good food. Many different children's perspective of good food is something simple and easy like pizza. In America, the commonly ordered foods at birthday parties are pizza, burgers, pasta, salad, chips, and fried chicken. The beverages used in these parties are mainly soda, juice and other drinks of these types. Alcohol is not consumed by children, thus should be avoided by all means. This means that alcoholic drinks are not catered at birthday party for kids. There are some cases where there is but, it is securely only served for the adults attending the party. Pleasing children when it comes to food is not as hard, all they really do expect is to be served a variety of foods, usually junk food. Serving food that the kids and the people attending it would like is what is needed in the catering business. Some kids would like to have unique food. For example, some might want Chinese food while some might prefer Italian food. It is essential to make sure and run these decisions along with your client prior to making the actual meals.

Most caterers charge all birthday parties by how much food is demanded. Also, many times they recommend how the birthday party should be handled and how the food style should be. This is a great way that you can set yourself different from other competition. By being able to provide more services than just catering, you can easily set yourself apart and be remembered. By having a fun staff to help you at these events is an extremely important aspect, since they need to be active and keep up with the rest of the children's demands.

Birthday Parties For Adults

Birthday parties are some of the profitable caterings which the catering industry covers. Adults want a good caterer to cater the party with good food and beverages. The food that is usually used in the birthday parties for adults consist of sandwiches, chicken, cocktails, seafood, pasta and a large variety of beverages, most notably alcoholic beverages. Wine, champagne, beer, scotch, and whisky are the most commonly used alcoholic drinks at adult birthday parties. The service that is provided for the party is very important as well. The food, as usual is also very important.

The Focus Is On The Food And Service

Success in the kitchen begins with learning how to read cooking recipes. Learning to read and cook a recipe is a great way to process how to blend the different flavors found in food. While it may seem obvious, learning to read a recipe is a very beneficial household skill that many people take for granted. The most important thing to remember when cooking a new recipe is to read the recipe entirely, all the way through, from beginning to end. Many people do not perform this initial step and often have a frustrating time in the kitchen because of this oversight.

Recipe Familiarity

The main reason it is so important to read a recipe from beginning to end is to become familiar with all of the steps involved in cooking the recipe. Knowing the overall directions of the recipe will make the cooking of it much easier. Often times a recipe will have specific directions for mixing the dry and liquid ingredients separately, prior to combining them. If the recipe is only read step-by-step, it is quite possible that the wet and dry ingredients will be combined in one bowl well before this should happen.

A Good Knowledge On Ingredients

Once you have read through the entire recipe, go back through and gather the various ingredients that are needed to make the finished product. This is a very valuable step as there is nothing worse than getting a halfway through the cooking of a recipe only to discover that you do not have all the necessary ingredients to complete the cooking process.

It is also important to make sure that you have the appropriate type of ingredients; prepared mustard is very different from dried mustard, just as baking soda and baking powder are very different. Making sure that all the proper ingredients are available and that you have the proper amounts called for, will make cooking the recipe much easier. There is nothing worse than getting halfway through the preparation of a recipe only to discover you do not have enough ingredients to finish cooking the recipe.

Basic Cooking Oils

Basically, when fat from a plant or animal is purified and kept at room temperature in the form of liquid, it is known as cooking oil. Naturally, this gives rise to many different kinds of cooking oil of which soybean, olive, peanut, sesame and rice bran oil, amongst others are good examples. There are some types of oil that are termed as vegetable oils and refer to cooking oil products that are a blend of different oils based on corn, soybean, and palm as well as sunflower oil.

Many Flavored Oils Are Also Available

Many cooking oils are flavored and this is achieved by immersing aromatic foods including peppers, herbs and more into the oil for a considerable period of time. You need to exercise care not to take in too much of these oils as it could adversely affect your health. No doubt, you need fats which are essential nutrients in a person's diet. However, a diet that is not well balanced will harm a person's health. Thus cooking oil has a special problem as there are trans fats created in the oils that form because of hydrogenation of oils and which are detrimental to a person's health.

Cooking oils are also sensitive to heat, light as well as being exposed to oxygen and you can tell when they have gone bad when they begin to give off a rancid smell and thus have greatly diminished nutrient value. A way to prevent the oil from turning rancid is to use what is known as tank blanketing. Otherwise, it is best to store these cooking oils in a refrigerator or in a cool and dry place.

There are many different types of cooking oil including canola oil, coconut oil, corn and cottonseed oil, grape seed oil as well as lard and much more. Each has different amounts of saturated fat and monosaturated as well as polyunsaturated fats, and they also reach smoking points at different temperatures. Thus, you may want to use different cooking oils for different uses are they for frying, baking, salad dressing, shortening or for simple cooking.

In fact, there is no real consensus about what the exact smoking points of many of the more popular cooking oils are and there is also no real standardization about how they are termed "refined". In any case, to help you decide on which the best cooking oils are, you could consider the fact that lighter as well as more refined oils are going to have higher smoking points. So, be careful to enquire about this aspect and ensure that you put out any burning oil fire prior to heating. Also, waste of these oils can be used to produce bio-diesel.

Equipment Needs

The third step is to gather all the necessary equipment that will be required in the preparation and cooking of the recipe. Insuring that you have a spring form pan prior to creating a cheese cake just makes good common sense but you would be surprised how a necessary piece of baking or cooking equipment can be overlooked and disrupt the whole cooking process.

Don't forget to familiarize yourself with cooking temperatures, preparation time, cooking time and any other particulars that are important to the successful cooking experience of your recipe.

Basic Cooking Equipment

Some cooks do not even look at a cookbook, and they make wonderful meals for a couple or a couple of hundred. These cooks appreciate good cooking equipment because this makes their jobs easier. There are many different pieces of cooking equipment that provide for the preparation of many different dishes. The cooking equipment in a chef's kitchen might consist of hundreds of pieces of cooking equipment. The cooking equipment starts with the major appliances in the kitchen. A good cook might have a kitchen with a couple of ovens and at least one sophisticated stovetop.

The cooking equipment will also include a wide variety of pots to make many different dishes. These pieces of cooking equipment will come in many different sizes from tiny pots to large soup pots. The pots in a kitchen might include several frying pans, stock pots, sauté pans and many other types. These pots will all have lids to make sure the dinner preparations can be covered if necessary. Some of the pots will be made with copper bottoms while others might be made of special metals that conduct the heat properly for even cooking. Many cooks are very particular about the types of pans used in their kitchens.

Cooking Equipment Is A Chef's Pride And Joy

An industrious cook will be careful in choosing their cooking equipment to make their job easier and better. The pots are an important element of kitchen equipment, but the pans are important to make special dishes. Most cooks will want to have a variety of pans for delicious cakes and tasty pies. There should be pans to make a spicy Mexican dish or a fine lasagna. A good cook will want to have some pans to make some brownies for a rich dessert. Other pans will be useful for muffins or casseroles.

Food preparation will be much easier with cooking equipment in different shapes and sizes. A food processor can shorten the time spent in the kitchen, and a blender can serve to mix substances quickly. Chopping and dicing can be done with the food processors and reduce the time a cook spends on these tasks. A sharp set of knives is essential to the work in any kitchen so many cooks choose their sets carefully. Some cooks do not need to measure any ingredients because they know their recipes, but most cooks have to measure the ingredients as they proceed. A set of measuring cups and spoons will help a cook follow a fantastic recipe.

Basic Cooking Tips

Basic cooking techniques are very important to learn as possessing this knowledge not only increases the ease in which cooking projects are completed but also increases the overall enjoyment of cooking

Cooking Techniques Are Universal In The World Of Fine Cuisine

Basic cooking techniques have specific names that are universal among cookbook authors, cooking schools and chefs. Learning these basic cooking methods and techniques are integral to successfully learning to cook.

A Definition Of Basic Cooking Techniques

Blanching or parboiling are two names that refer to one important cooking technique that is used to soften a vegetable. This step is usually done prior to moving forward with another cooking step, generally to ease the removal of vegetable skins or to leach out bitterness of certain vegetables. Often times, the vegetables are shocked, or plunged into a bowl of ice water to stop the vegetables from cooking any further.

Broiling is a term used to describe a particular method of cooking. This term refers to using high heat to brown food under direct heat. Some foods such as eggplant, croutons and tofu can be fully cooked under a broiler but for most others, it is a secondary cooking method used to brown or toast the tops of the foods. When using a broiler, it is important to keep foods between 4-6 inches from the heat source.

Steaming is a popular method of food preparation that promotes the healthy retention of nutrients. Steaming generally refers to the cooking of vegetables over a small amount of water. There are special steaming pots that can be purchased in kitchen stores designed specifically to fit into a pan. This specialty kitchen tool holds the vegetables above the water and maintains the quality of the steamed food.

Sautéing is a term that is used to describe the cooking of vegetables over high heat in a specially designed pan. Sauté is a term that is used to refer to the cooking method, a specifically designed pan and as a name or fashion of preparation such as "sautéed mushrooms".

Simmering and Boiling are two common terms used in everyday cooking terminology, both are very important forms of everyday cooking. Boiling is a term used to describe a fast way of completing food preparation without losing a great deal of nutrients. When boiling food, it is important to have a large rolling boil in the water prior to introducing the foods that are being cooked. Simmering is the preparation of food at a soft boil rather than the rolling, bubble breaking boil. There are many foods that required a cooking process that includes both boiling and simmering. It is important when cooking that the instructions following these two methods of cooking are followed precisely to insure that the food is prepared properly.

Cooking techniques are a very important part of learning to cook successfully. If you are interested in learning more about cooking techniques, it is possible to buy training cookbooks, cooking technique manuals and dictionaries to increase your overall knowledge of cooking.

Cooking Lobster

Nothing can be more elegant than a fabulous lobster dinner. Cooking lobster can be a challenge, but with the right preparation and supplies, this gourmet seafood can be cooked in your own home.

Selecting Supplies

The first step in cooking lobster is finding a good lobster steamer. A steamer fits inside of a bigger pot that is placed on a stovetop. When cooking lobster, a lid that is almost airtight is needed to properly steam the lobster. Boiling is another suggestion for cooking lobster. A very large deep pot is needed for this. All types of lobster pots can be purchased at many local stores or even on-line.

Choices In Cooking Lobster

There are several ways to cook lobster and retain the flavor. The first and probably best known is steaming. Salt is an important ingredient when cooking this type of seafood. Make sure there is about one tablespoon of salt for every quart of water. Favorite herbs that can be added include garlic, bay leaf or peppercorn. In addition, adding an onion can add flavor to the cooking lobster.

There is some thought that lobsters can be hypnotized before being placed in a steamer or boiling water. Rub the lobster on the stomach gently to hypnotize it. Before doing that, be sure that the claws are tapped tightly shut, to avoid lobster accidents. Live lobsters can also be killed before cooking. Using a very sharp knife and holding the lobster down by its tail; place the knife about an inch from its eyes to its tail. Press the knife in and then down towards its eyes. This is possibly the most humane way to kill the lobster.

Cooking lobsters by boiling is a tried and true method. It is similar to steaming, in that spices and salt can be added to the water. Steaming takes a little less time than boiling. Cooking lobster through boiling takes about five minutes per pound.

For the more adventurous gourmet, there are even more recipes that involve cooking lobster. The Lobster Bisque soup is a very popular choice. Cooking lobster to make bisque, takes time and there are many good recipes to be found. Additional recipes for cooking lobster include, Lobster Chili, Lobster Rolls and Lobster Thermidor among others.

Finding recipes for cooking lobster is easy, they can be found on-line and at any bookstore.

Discovering the fine art of cooking lobster can expand any budding chiefs experience and creates a flavorful meal.

Cooking Crab Legs

Many people view cooking crab legs as a difficult task too great to be done by a novice chief at home. There is nothing further from the truth. Cooking crab legs is a simple process that really doesn't take long.

Why Is Cooking Crab Legs So Easy?

Crab legs that are sold in markets across the country, are already cooked. The reason for this is that when the crabs are caught, they are then cooked on board the ship. Immediately after cooking they are flash frozen. This helps seal in the flavor. Because of this process, cooking crab legs is very simple.

When purchasing crab legs, be sure to check and see if they have been thawed. Thawed out crab legs will sometimes lose their taste and freshness. When determining how many crab legs should be purchased, figure on about one pound per person. This should supply everyone with enough meat from the crab legs. Crab legs can be kept in the refrigerator up to two days after they have thawed. It is best to begin cooking crab legs right after they have thawed out.

Choices In Cooking Crab Legs

There are several successful methods to cooking crab legs. One that is extremely popular is the traditional steaming method. This will require a large pot and a steamer fixture that can be placed in the pot. An airtight lid is recommended in order to steam the crab legs quickly. Add about one tablespoon of salt for every two cups of water. When cooking crab legs with this method, it generally takes five to seven minutes to cook them.

Baking is another method to cooking crab legs. Heat the oven to about 350 degrees. Crack the crab legs and brush them with butter. Bake for about eight to nine minutes.

Boiling crab legs is a method that can be used if you have managed to find uncooked crab legs. In a large pot, place about one tablespoon of salt and bring the water to a boil. Drop the crab legs in and boil for about five to seven minutes. Drain the water and rinse the crab legs with cold water. They are then ready to serve.

Crab legs can even be cooked in a microwave. Wrap the crab legs in a moist paper towel. Cook for two to three minutes.

Cooking crab legs is very easy. They can be made quickly and with little fuss, allowing for more time to enjoy this tender delicious meal.

Cooking Ribs

Until three years ago I had never cooked ribs. I do not enjoy messy eating and I never saw anyone eat ribs in a tidy fashion. Therefore, when I began cooking for my family I managed to never cook ribs for dinner. In fact, I never even knew that my husband and stepchildren enjoyed eating ribs.

Then, One day my husband asked me why I never cooked ribs for dinner. It took me a moment to realize that he was serious. This was the first time he had ever asked me to cook ribs. So, after a long pause I explained that I really saw no reason to cook ribs. I explained that I found them to be messy, annoying and really there was very little meat on the bones. He explained that he would like to have ribs cooked for dinner one day. I told him to go ahead. That conversation took place ten years ago and for seven years no ribs were cooked in my house.

A Cookware Party Changed My Mind About Cooking Ribs

One day I went to a cookware party that specialized in stoneware. At the party one of the item for sale was a very expensive stoneware roaster. The hostess explained how the stoneware roaster cooked food to perfection, working somewhat like a stone bar-b-que dug into the ground at parties and pig roasts. I decided I would buy the roaster and give it a try after all hadn't my husband said he wanted me to start cooking ribs.

Cooking Ribs For My Family Provides Quite The Surprise

I followed the directions for cooking ribs; one rack of ribs, family's favorite barbecue sauce and 10-12 hours in the oven at 250 degrees, simple enough. I put the entire combination together and left for work. When I returned home that evening, my house smelled like a Hawaiian luau. The smoky barbecue and beef mingled in the air in an aroma that made everyone's mouth water. Served with fresh pineapple, baked potatoes and a fresh green salad on the side, I came to realize what my husband found so delightful in a plate of cooked ribs.

Stoneware Roaster Cooks Like An Expensive Barbecue Pit, Only Better

I will tell you that the stoneware roaster that I bought cooked the ribs to perfection. The meat literally fell off of the bones. It was tender, tasty and perfectly roasted. To this day my husband may complain amount the money I spend but he never complains about that roaster I bought.

Cooking Steak

Cooking steak can be a wonderful treat for family and friends. There are so many different types of steak, and each cook will probably have some favorite cuts. Some cooks will choose to have a sirloin cut because these cuts are tender, juicy and usually a great entrée for a special meal. The person in charge of the meal might decide that cooking steak should start with rib eye steak which is a cut that provides a tasty meal for all those at the table. Chateaubriand steak is a favorite for those who are cooking steak for two. This cut is a very tasty piece of meat.

Those cooks who decide that cooking steak is a great idea for the next meal will want to confer with the diners to see how they would like their steak done by the chef. Some people want their steak very rare, and this type of order will result in very pink meat in the middle of the steak when it is ready to serve. Those diners who like their steak medium rare will end up with a steak that is brown on the outside and red on the inside. Those diners who like their steaks well done will be served a piece of meat that is completely brown inside and out.

Different Methods Can Be Used When Cooking Steak

Cooking steak can be done inside or outside depending on the weather and the available facilities. Those cooks who are intent on cooking steak outdoors will probably have a fine grill for the job. There are gas grills that can be used although many people like to have a steak grilled over charcoal. The later method gives a very special taste to the meat. Cooking steak is often done inside under a broiler or in a frying pan. Some people use certain types of steak ground into hamburgers.

Many people immediately think of beef when the word steak is mentioned, but there are other types of steak that can make delicious meals. There are fish steaks that are often very nutritious and great for those on a diet. Lamb steaks are also very delicious when prepared by a talented cook, and these often have less fat than the beef steaks.

Cooking steak for a group of family and friends is often a welcome venture whether the steak is fish, beef or lamb. The preparation can make a significant difference in the taste of a steak.

Low Fat Cooking

There may be many new diet cooking fads that may grab your attention and which you may consider using. However, to play safe it would be better to check out the low fat cooking recipes before making a decision. The reason for checking out low fat cooking recipes are that there are many meals that you can cook up that still have great taste in spite of being low fat dishes, and they are also cost beneficial to you.

Lower The Amount Of Fatty Foods

It is not uncommon for regular users of low fat cooking to know their recipes by heart and enjoy the many benefits of such meals such as lowering the amount of fatty foods that are consumed. If you can source the right low fat cooking recipes and make the effort to learn about different tips on this method of cooking, you will not miss the fat-filled meals that you have given up on.

The first thing you need to remember is to use cooking spray as the staple of your low fat cooking routines, which are readily available and also come in different varieties of flavors while also not adding fat to your preparations.

These cooking sprays are ideal substitutes for butter as well as oil and help in considerably reducing fat content in your meals.

You would also appreciate using fish for your low fat cooking meals and it is possible to cook up some wonderful fish dishes in quick time, and all you will need is some foil and placing flounder in the middle and spraying with cooking spray while also adding favored vegetables and baking in an oven. There is nothing more to this simple low fat cooking preparation.

Besides chicken and fish, it is also possible to use red meats in your low fat cooking recipes though such meats would generally be tough as compared with the fatter meats, though this problem is easily solved by using a tenderizer. Other ingredients that you can use include spices and condiments such as lemon and honey as also use peppers and seasoning. With these ingredients, you will find your low fat cooking to be enjoyable and you won't also miss your fatty foods that will also help to control your calorie intakes.

However, this is not to say that you should eliminate all fat from your diet as that would make your meals very bland as well as boring. Just like your automobile engine requires oil to run, your body too requires limited doses of fat and oil. The bottom line is that if you use your low fat cooking preparations and include no more than thirty percent fat, it would lead to reducing risk of heart disease, as well as some forms of cancer and diabetes as well.

Cooking Asparagus

When thinking about cooking asparagus, preparation is the key whether it will be cooked by boiling, steaming, grilling or roasting. Asparagus can also be cooked in the microwave, cut into sections to be used in stir fry and can be blanched to use with vegetable dips. The fresher the asparagus the better it will taste and when bought in the store in can be maintained for two or three days, if stored properly.

Trimming asparagus is best done by hand by simply bending the stalk until it breaks. If it bends but will not snap it is probably old and may not have a fresh flavor. When preparing for cooking asparagus some cooks will peel the outer layer. While this not necessary, it can help with the tenderness of the stalks. While it is the fibers inside the outer layer that need softened when cooking asparagus, it is good to peel only a couple of spots on the outside. This will allow enough steam to the inside to cook thoroughly.

To peel prior to cooking asparagus, lay the stalk flat on the counter or cutting board and using a vegetable peeler start at the top and peel toward the end. It can be peeled completely but to save time, removing one portion of the peel from each side will suffice.

Stalks Should Face Same Direction While Cooking
Asparagus

One the stalks have been peeled and trimmer to the
desired size, they can be placed in a saucepan with about
one inch of water in the bottom. The asparagus can be
trimmed at the bottom to fit into the saucepan so they
stand vertical. Tie them together with kitchen string to
help the bundle stand upright and to evenly steam the
entire bundle. It may be wise to use two strings when
cooking asparagus, one at the top and one near the bottom
to keep them secured. Depending on thickness, five to 10
minutes should be enough.

When cooking asparagus by boiling, use just enough water
to cover the asparagus, having all the stems pointing in the
same direction, keeping them covered with water. It will
take four to six minutes to cook completely. To grill, place
a cooking screen over the fire or skewers can be used to
keep the spears from falling through the grate. It only
takes about 30 seconds to 60 minutes, depending on the
thickness when cooking asparagus over the grill.

For cooking asparagus by roasting, they can be laid flat on
a baking sheet and put in the oven at 425 degrees for two
to three minutes. This provides a still tender stalk with a
special roasted taste. Use salt or other seasonings to taste.

Cooking Corned Beef

Corned beef and cabbage is considered a traditional Irish feast. Many want to copy this recipe to create this meal to celebrate St. Patrick's Day. Finding a good recipe that is easy to follow can be tricky, but this cooking corned beef recipe requires little assistance.

The First Step In Cooking Corned Beef

For all cooking projects it is important to make sure that all the essential utensils are in supply. Check for measuring cups, spoons, dicing knives and a pan to cook the meal in. When cooking corned beef, selecting a cut of meat is important.

The term "corned" is used as a reference to the way the meat has been cured. Before refrigeration, meat was cured with salt in rows referred to as "corns". The beef brisket is cured today with salt water to give it the traditional taste of a corned cured beef.

Before cooking corned beef, check the dates on the package before selecting a package of corned beef. It is important to purchase a package that is fresh. A well sealed package of corned beef can be frozen for up to one month. After cooking corned beef, the leftovers are fresh for 3 to4 days.

To make the corned beef as tender as possible, it may require a long cooking time for the corned beef. Cooking corned beef can be done in the oven, with a slow cooker or on the stove. Again, this is a cut of meat that needs to be cooked for a long time. Corned beef can still be slightly pink, even if it is cooked completely.

If cooking corned beef in the oven, make sure to place the meat fat side up. It should be cooked at around 350 degrees. Cover it with some water, around an inch. It generally takes about an hour for each pound of meat.

Cooking corned beef in a crock pot, will enable vegetables to be cooked at the same time. Just place the vegetables on the bottom first. Next, cut the corned beef in pieces to allow for the complete cooking of the corned beef. Next add water, about one cup. This type of cooking can take up to 10-12 hours.

If cooking corned beef on the stove is the option, place the meat fat side up in a large pan. Cover it with water and then bring the water to a boil. Reduce heat and simmer for one hour per pound of meat.

Cooking corned beef is simple and creates a traditional family feast to be enjoyed by everyone.

Diabetic Cooking

Diabetes is a very serious disease, but those afflicted with this condition can take precautions to improve their health. Diabetic cooking is one way that people with this dread disease can improve their health. Those with diabetes do not have to stick to bland food if they have meals prepared with diabetic cooking essentials. Diabetic cooking should concentrate on healthy meals that are full of nutritious ingredients. Diabetic cooking does not have to exclude all the regular favorites, but it may require some exclusions. Diabetic cooking does not have to be very complicated. Following some basic rules should provide for healthy eating.

Diabetic cooking should have plenty of vegetables, fruits and whole grains for nutritious meals. Some excellent planning should make for some delicious yet healthy meals for a diabetic and all of their family members. Good planning can provide for excellent meals that the whole family will enjoy. Most of the family members will not even realize that they are eating diabetic cooking if the meals are planned and prepared well. Diabetic cooking will be good for the diabetic member and great for all of the other family members as well. Those people who follow the rules for diabetic cooking will probably lose some weight or maintain their healthy weight.

Diabetic Cooking Does Not Require Complicated Menus

Diabetics should try to stick to a regular schedule for their meals and snacks if possible. Each person with diabetes should consult with their doctor about their condition and the eating requirements. Some doctors may suggest that the diabetic lose weight although others will just have to eat nutritious meals throughout the day. Those diabetics that need to lose some weight should get some suggestions from their doctor. Most diabetic diets recommend a set number of servings that include the major food groups.

Diabetic cooking should account for the carbohydrates in the meals throughout the day. There is information about carbohydrates on the label of each food product so this should not be difficult to calculate. A careful balance of the carbohydrates in a meal will help those with diabetes. Plenty of starches are a great addition to keep a diabetic healthy. These can be added to the diet with cereal and bread. Most diabetics will have to cut out the sweets so people will want to think of some creative desserts. There are so many fruits that can be a wonderful end to a delicious meal.

Healthy Cooking

The need to eat healthy food should always be uppermost in mind, which means more than simply changing eating habits and involves changing the method of cooking at home. In fact, healthy cooking at home is not just about concocting bland or boring dishes, and can even lead to flavored dishes that mean you can continue to eat well as also feel well with such preparations.

Leaner Meat Cuts

Healthy cooking involves choosing leaner cuts of meat such as low fat chicken and fish, though some other meats can also be chosen that do not contain high amount of fat. You could choose sirloin and round cuts when selecting your red meats and you must also ensure that you check and buy only meat that has low marbling and the fat content should also be trimmed off prior to cooking. You should also choose ground beef that is as much as ninety-five percent lean when moving over to healthy cooking habits.

Also, to get around the problem of lean meat drying out easily, you could include in your healthy cooking some marinade that are more useful than just to flavor the food. In addition, it is also possible for you to add acidic liquids that can easily decompose the connective tissue of the meat. There are many low fat marinades to choose from and you can also prepare it yourself. Marinating for about twenty minutes should be sufficient for average sized meat cuts and yogurt is wonderful for chicken that can be used for eight hours and even left overnight.

You might be thinking that healthy cooking means having to only eat bland vegetables. This is not true as you can sauté your vegetables using tiny quantities of chicken broth and even vegetable broth as a substitute for oil, and also use a few herbs and chopped chives to get the vegetables to have a new as well as zestful taste. Another alternative you can use when healthy cooking is to roast vegetables because root vegetables as well as firm vegetables will turn out much better.

Healthy cooking also does not mean having to do without your dessert since you can always eat fruits as part of wonderful dessert dishes, or even as a side dish to your meal. Mixed berries with a topping of fat free vanilla yogurt will do very well for your taste buds, and keep you healthy as well. Bananas that have been sautéed are another good option for you.

Sure, it is important to live healthy, but with some innovations and changes, your healthy cooking can provide you with a better as well as healthier meal that will not have you hankering for those unhealthy foods that you have been trying so hard to give up.

Looking to get your hands on more great books?

Come visit us on the web and check out our great collection of books covering all categories and topics. We have something for everyone.

http://www.kmspublishing.com